# The Saturn Rocket

by Zoë Clarke
illustrated by Ally Marie

Nish had ten books on Saturn.

He had a chart showing the planets.

I will get to Saturn!

I need a rocket
to get there.

Look in the shed for boxes.

The shed was a mess.
The boxes were near the back.

Nish cut out some wings.
He cut out a tail.

He cut windows in the boxes.
Then he got some red paint.

This rocket will get me there!

Nish got in his rocket.
He ran down the garden.

The wings fell off!
The tail fell off!
Nish was sad.

Nish had a hug.

Dad took Nish to the rooftop.

Mum had set up something cool!

Nish took a look at the night.

I will get a rocket to Saturn. Wait and see!

Encourage students to use the pictures to retell the story.